I0797918

Published by arrangement with Loewe Verlag GmbH.

Title of the original German edition: *Sicher im Netz!*

Sky Pony Press books may be purchased in bulk at special discounts for sales promotion, corporate gifts, fund-raising, or educational purposes. Special editions can also be created to specifications. For details, contact the Special Sales Department, Sky Pony Press, 307 West 36th Street, 11th Floor, New York, NY 10018 or info@skyhorsepublishing.com.

Visit our website at www.skyponypress.com.

10 9 8 7 6 5 4 3 2 1

Manufactured in China, 2025
This product conforms to CPSIA 2008

Library of Congress Cataloging-in-Publication Data is available on file.

Cover design by Ramona Karl & Kai Texel
Cover illustrations by Nikolai Renger

US Edition edited by Nicole Frail

Print ISBN: 978-1-5107-7711-8
Ebook ISBN: 978-1-5107-7712-5

How Can I Be Safe Online?

Learning How to Behave and Protect Myself on the Internet

Written by
Dagmar Geisler

Illustrated by
Nikolai Renger

Translated by
Andy Berasaluce

Sky Pony Press
New York

FiGHT!

Table of Contents

Madison and Luke Know the Internet

Madison and Luke are best friends and *Web Experts*.
That's what the others in their class say,
and what Ms. Schwarz, the teacher, says too.
The two of them once made a list that contains everything you need to know before doing a video conference.[1]
Ms. Schwarz then tried it out with her students.
Thanks to Madison and Luke, everything worked out great.

1 *You can read about it in the book: Using the Internet for Virtual School*

Because they've thought so much about how to interact with others online, the two are now giving a presentation. They talk about the importance of being kind online and tell the story of Luke's big brother, Till, and his girlfriend, Aylin. The two of them gave permission first to have their story shared. "It's for a good cause," they said.

That Time Till Freaked Out

Till had a huge crush on Aylin. So huge that, for a long time, he didn't dare tell her. And then there was a time when it seemed like Aylin would never want to have anything to do with him again. That was the day Till got into real trouble because of the Internet.

Till’s best friend, Ali, was angry because the website was for their shared research project. Till was supposed to be the presenter. Many people online made fun of him. And that's when Till freaked out. He wrote back a lot of nasty things.

Some words were so disgusting that he would never say them in real life. But he wrote them. Out of sheer anger, Till didn't even notice that there was also a person commenting who actually just wanted to be nice. He just kept spewing swear words.

The nice person was Aylin. Till hadn't noticed because, online, she called herself flikflak13. Till also had a Username but Aylin knew who was behind it.

This was pretty bad because the horrible words hurt Aylin a lot. She didn't want anything to do with Till anymore.

Things still ended well because Madison spoke to Aylin. She explained the whole thing to her. Aylin then reconciled with Till. Recently, the two have even been dating.

But first Aylin wanted Till to apologize to the others whom he insulted so badly. And that's what he did.

THE WEB-EXPERTS SAY:

We should be at least as friendly on the Internet as in real life. Nasty words hurt a lot. Online, where everyone can read them, they are even worse.

The presentation went over well. They got a good grade. And Ms. Schwarz said again that Luke and Madison are true *WEB EXPERTS.*

But then something dumb happened...

Oh, How Embarrassing!

When Madison and Luke first met, they were still in diapers. And there are a lot of photos of the two of them.

They recently retook some of the photos just for fun.

Madison took pictures with her mom's tablet.

And because she found the pictures so funny, Madison sent them to her friend, Steffi. Steffi is a little older and already has her own smartphone.

Steffi also thought they were funny and sent one of the photos to her friend. The worst possible photo to send, where Madison loses her bathing suit bottom in the kiddie pool.

To someone who doesn't know the story,

it looks like Madison just wanted to show people her BUTT.

And suddenly, a whole lot of people know about this photo. It's being sent around more and more, and some people even write silly captions and comments about it.

It has already landed on Till's phone.

It was *so embarassing.*

The picture wasn't meant for the whole world, just Madison and Luke.

“You shouldn’t have sent it to Steffi,” says Luke.

“I know that now,” Madison grumbles. She would love to go hide in a cave and never come out.

And she's totally mad at Steffi. How could she just send it to someone else?

But it happened, and it can't be taken back now.

“Well,” says Madison. “The Web-Experts have learned something again.”

“You said it,” replies Luke.

THE WEB-EXPERTS SAY:

 Online, we only show or write things that we would show or say in the middle of the schoolyard in broad daylight. Anything else can be quite embarrassing, or even dangerous.

 We only send pictures and messages from someone else with their permission.

 We have a right to our own image. There's even a law about it.

Aylin Gets Upset

The next afternoon, they meet in Luke's garden. Till is also there, practicing walking on a slackline.

Suddenly, Aylin comes storming into the garden.

She is bright red in the face and very angry.

"ARE YOU CRAZY?" she screams.

Till falls off the rope in shock.

“What’s wrong?” he calls, rubbing his sore behind.

“You’re asking that?” Aylin shouts. “You’re just going to break up with me? And by a stupid chat message? You don’t have the guts to say it to my face?"

"Huh?" says Till.

"Don't pretend now!" Aylin puts her hands at her sides. "You just wrote to me yourself."

"I did? When?" Till stammers. He grabs his head, even though he didn't fall on it. Or did he?

Aylin pulls her phone out of her pocket and taps it. "Here, five minutes ago."

All four lean over the screen. Aylin now has tears in her eyes.

"I was so happy when you made this chat for the two of us."

She sniffles. "I thought that was really cute. And now?"

"What chat?" Till croaks.

"Well, this one." Aylin opens the chat history. It was filled with photos.

Till spray-painting a heart with "Aylin" in it on the wall. Till with a huge bouquet of roses, Till in a heart made of candles. There's also a bunch of cuddly stuff there too. Luke rolls his eyes. "But that's not me." Till's voice can hardly be heard anymore. "What are you saying?" Aylin's voice is also very hoarse now.

"That can't be," says Madison.
"Didn't you realize that it came from a completely different cell number?" asks Luke.
"Yes," says Aylin. "But I didn't think anything of it. Except that Till might also have a tablet."

Aylin has a suspicion about who might have done it. Robin from her sports club, who really wants to date her, and is terribly jealous of Till.
"But the photos look totally real," says Madison. Aylin nods. Robin's pretty good at this sort of thing.

THE WEB-EXPERTS SAY:

 Some people write using fake names online, pretending to be younger or older.

 They beautify themselves or they use a photo of someone else.

 Photos and videos can be altered or faked entirely.

 In television news, many people work around the clock to find out whether Internet news is real or fake. If it takes them so much effort, how are we supposed to be sure?

 Ideally: We don't believe everything we read or see online!

 And also: If someone we know suddenly uses a different number, we don't answer until we're absolutely sure it's the same person.

Actually, everything is fine between Aylin and Till now. Though the two still bicker a little. Aylin is really disappointed that all the sweet talk about love was fake.

"Really? That's what you're into?" asks Till, shaking his head. But before the two get into an argument, Till's friend Ali comes whizzing up on his bike. Brakes squealing, he stops and shouts: "It's a good thing you're here. I need your advice!"

Something's Wrong

Ali loves to play computer games. He's really good at them. His opponents are scattered across the country, and he has even become a bit friendly with some. They send each other short messages and talk about the game.

One boy wrote Ali particularly often. And they very quickly started to chat about other things as well. They sent each other photos and videos and a lot of jokes.

"But now it's getting kind of weird," says Ali.

"He thinks I'm good-looking, and he's asking for my address so he can send me a surprise."

"That's sweet," says Aylin. "You are really good-looking." Till looks at her in surprise.

"Thank you," Ali says. "But that's not the point. I'm just not sure I'm truly chatting with a boy my age anymore."

"Right," says Till. "The address thing is kind of suspicious."

"Exactly," says Ali. "But it's mean if I'm suspicious of him and he just really wants to be nice."

"Tell him you're happy to talk to him about the game, but nothing else," Aylin says.

"What if he gets offended?" asks Ali.

"Anyone who's offended because you're protecting yourself isn't that nice after all," says Aylin.

THE WEB-EXPERTS SAY:

 It's best to talk online only with friends we know in real life.

 When dealing with someone we don't really know, like while playing a game, we don't talk about anything other than the game.

 We don't send photos of ourselves.

 No videos, either.

 Under no circumstances do we send our address.

 We don't say which school we go to, or which clubs we play for or belong to.

 There are just people who want to take advantage of others on the Internet.

 That's not nice. But that's how it is.

 In order to be safe on the Internet, we have to pay attention to this.

Who Does Something Like That?

The five of them talk for a while about what you can come across on the Internet. Back home in the evening, Madison's head is buzzing from all this.

She asks if she can watch some *cat videos* on her mom's phone. It's so cozy at home on the sofa. Madison drinks a cup of cocoa and laughs her head off. Some cats come up with the funniest ideas.

She clicks on a video of a black and white cat and watches as he tries to steal food from the family dog's bowl. In the next video, she sees a tiny kitten playing with a ball of wool. Madison sighs pleasantly and clicks on a picture of a particularly cute, fluffy tabby cat.

But she probably shouldn't have done that.

Madison is completely taken aback. A few people can be seen, wearing their caps pulled low over their faces, torturing the poo little animal. Madison hears the cat's desperate cries and watches as what the people do becomes more and more cruel.

This can't be real!

Madison thinks Luke, Till, Aylin, and Ali should also know about this. And because she has already sent something to her friends on her mom's phone a few times, she quickly sends the video to Till and Aylin, asking them to show Luke and Ali too.

She doesn't tell her mom about it at first. She can already imagine that Mama wouldn’t let her use the phone so readily anymore if she knew how easy it is to see horrible things there, even if you weren't even looking for them.

The friends meet the next day right after school. Aylin is outraged by the malice of the video, and has already sent the video of the tortured cat to her friends, who are all just as angry about the animal abusers.

"What can we do?" asks Madison. A heated discussion ensues. Till thinks it would've been good if Madison had spoken to her mother right away.

"It's easy for you to talk," Madison says. "I have to beg for every minute that I use her phone."

Ali thinks it may not have been a good idea to forward the video.

"What for? Are you worried about nightmares?" asks Till.

"I think I know what Ali means," says Luke. "If we keep sharing this type of crap, these criminals get exactly what they want. Clicks and more clicks. And a lot of clicks bring money."

"You mean they torture the cat to get money?" Madison just can't believe it.

"It's quite possible," says Ali. "Money or attention. And we don't want to give them either."

"And we don't want that kind of trash to clutter our *brains*," Aylin says. "I couldn't fall asleep last night because I kept hearing the little cat's cries."

"I'm sorry," says Madison. "I didn't want that."

"No need to feel sorry," replies Aylin. "I forwarded the video too, because I was so shocked, but I won't do that in the future."

"But what do we do then?" asks Till.

THE WEB-EXPERTS SAY:

 We talk to the adults we trust. They need to know that we need them so that we are not left alone with horrible things on the Internet.

 We can tell adults anything, without having to be afraid that they'll take the cell phone away from us out of caution or not give us one at all.

We don't send anything like that video to others.

Because we don't want to scare anyone ourselves.

Because we don't want people who put something like that online to make money from it or get a lot of attention.

If we know how to, the most we can do is take a Screenshot[2] to show it to an adult.

By the way, we aren't cowards because we don't want to look at anything awful. We just think that the bad guys should keep it to themselves.

If we've eaten something bad, our bodies can get rid of it. But unfortunately, our brains can't puke.

So let's keep our brains safe. That's easy.

2 *A Screenshot is a photo of what can be seen on the screen.*

"Wow!" says Luke. "Why don't you need a driver's license to use the Internet? There's so much to keep in mind."

"Oh, man!" says Till. "Before you get any more brilliant ideas, little brother, I'll take you all for some ice cream. I still have some money left from delivering newspapers."

Till is very generous. Everyone gets two scoops from the best ice cream shop in town.

"Mmm, delicious," says Madison. "Eating ice cream is almost my favorite thing to do."

"And best of all," says Luke, "you don't even have to go online for it."

Advice and Help

CyberTipline
www.report.cybertip.org/
(800) 843-5678 (24-7 Call Center)

iKeepSafe
www.ikeepsafe.org
(202) 505-4408
info@ikeepsafe.org

Family Online Safety Institute
www.fosi.org/
400 7th Street NW
Suite 306
Washington, DC, DC 20004, US

Connect Safely
www.connectsafely.org/
linktr.ee/connectsafely

Love146
www.love146.org/
203.772.4420
notanumber@love146.org

Shared Hope International

https://sharedhope.org/what-we-do/prevent/awareness/internetsafety/

(866) 437-5433

Stop Bullying – Cyberbullying

https://www.stopbullying.gov/cyberbullying/how-to-report

NetSmartz

https://www.missingkids.org/netsmartz/home

Afterword

When I was a child, there was no Internet and I sometimes imagine how fascinated I would have been by a miracle box like the smartphone.

It is just as indispensable in today's world as roads. With road traffic, we have found rules that help us navigate it as safely as possible. We've developed a sense of when we can trust our children to find their way around on their own.

The Internet is still relatively new and, therefore, we must learn to both recognize its dangers and find a set of rules that protect ourselves and our children from their effects.

This set of rules cannot only consist of prohibitions and avoidance. That doesn't work for traffic either. But the way in which we slowly introduce our children to it could offer a blueprint that we can similarly apply to using the Internet.

Offer patient support for as long as necessary.

Educate about the possible dangers without causing fear. Great openness makes it possible for children to ask questions and for adults to inform about what's going on, in both a positive and negative sense.

Richard David Precht once said, "I keep my brain safe." Our children have this right too. And I hope that they not only learn to say, "My body belongs to me!" but also "My brain and soul belong to me! I won't be tempted to let just any trash inside." It is our job to support and encourage them in this.

Dagmar Geisler

Dagmar Geisler has already supported several generations of parents in guiding their children through emotionally difficult situations. Through her "Safe Child, Happy Parent" picture book series, the author sensitively covers the most important topics surrounding growing up: from body awareness to exploring your own emotional world to social interaction. Her work always includes a serving of humor. Especially when the topic is serious. Her books have been translated into twenty languages and also published in the United States.

Nikolai Renger was born in Karlsruhe and studied Visual Communication at the HFG in Pforzheim. He works as a freelance illustrator for various publishers and agencies and has been working at Atelier Remise in Karlsruhe since 2013.